Government in Papua New Guinea

SOCIAL SCIENCE PUPIL BOOK

Published by Department of Education Papua New Guinea

First Published 1987
Reprinted 1988, 1993, 1994, 1995, 1996 (twice), 1997, 1998 (twice), 1999, 2000 (twice), 2002, 2008 (twice), 2015(D)

ISBN 9980 58046 1
ISBN 978 9980 58046 7
National Library of Papua New Guinea

Typeset by Syarikat Seng Teik Sdn. Bhd., Malaysia
Printed in Australia by Ligare Pty Ltd
Published by Department of Education, Papua New Guinea
Prepared by Oxford University Press
253 Normanby Road, South Melbourne, Australia

Acknowledgements

This book was written by Carol Kidu. The Papua New Guinea Department of Education acknowledges the contribution of many individuals at the Curriculum Unit and on the Social Science Syllabus Advisory Committee to the trialling and review of the book. The participation of the teachers and students at the trial schools—Mongop, Laloki, Tapini, Kimbe, Goroka, Muaina, Kilakila, Badihagwa, and Gerehu Provincial High Schools—is greatly appreciated.

The textbook development work was co-ordinated by the late Greg Chariton, in the earlier stages, and subsequently by Mike McRory, Senior Curriculum Officer for Social Science at the Curriculum Unit.

The publisher wishes to thank the following people and organisations for supplying, and granting permission to reproduce, photographs:
Carol Kidu pp. 1, 3 (right), 4, 5, 9, 20, 50; Curriculum Unit, Papua New Guinea, pp. 3 (left); Niugini Nius pp. 15 (top), 33 (photographs of Mr Kwarara); Papua New Guinea Archives pp. 16, 18, 19; Hebamo Press pp. 24 (top),39, 40; Word Publishing pp. 33 (photographs of Messrs Chan, Momis, Okuk, Somare, Torato, Wingti); Post Courier pp.35, 38 (bottom).

Secretary's Message

The topic **Government in Papua New Guinea** is the fourth term's work in the Grade Seven Provincial High School Social Science Course. It is the first of the four topics which develop the theme **Government and People** through Grades Seven to Ten.

The book is the core learning material for the topic. A supporting set of teaching notes is available. The teaching notes advise the teachers on how to make the best use of the pupil's book.

The material in the book integrates the presentation of information, the development of ideas, reinforcement and application of Social Science skills and the fostering of attitudes.

Three types of activities appear at the end of each section. There are Exercises to ensure comprehension of the material; there are Things to Discuss and Things to Do. The activities combine work on sections of the book with direct investigations both inside and outside school.

This book is one of the items of instructional material produced for Provincial High Schools in Papua New Guinea as part of the Education III Textbook Sub-Project.

S G ROAKEINA
Secretary for Education

Contents

1. ***What is Government?*** ***1***
   - Two types of government 3
   - The work of government 4
   - Summary of main ideas 5
   - Activities 6

2. ***Traditional Government*** ***7***
   - Traditional government 7
   - Summary of main ideas 12
   - Activities 13

3. ***Local Government Councils and Community Government*** ***14***
   - History 14
   - Local government during colonial times 15
   - The growth and work of Local Government Councils 18
   - Changes in local government since Independence 20
   - Summary of main ideas 21
   - Activities 22

4. ***The Government of Large Groups*** ***23***
   - Preparing for Independence 24
   - The work of government 25
   - The legislative branch of government: Parliament 27
   - Summary of main ideas 30
   - Activities 31

5. ***National Parliament*** ***32***
   - How is Parliament organised? 32
   - The work of National Parliament 36
   - A visit to National Parliament 38
   - Summary of main ideas 40
   - Activities 41

6. ***Provincial Government*** ***42***
   - History 42
   - Opinions about provincial government 43
   - The structure of provincial government 44
   - Responsibilities of provincial government 45
   - Provincial government throughout the nation 46
   - Urban areas 49
   - Summary of main ideas 50
   - Activities 51

7. ***Conclusion*** ***52***
   - Activities 52

Glossary ***54***

Index ***56***

1. What is Government?

Ovia comes from a Motu village in the Central Province. Like most young people his age, he is not very interested in government. Government does not seem to be important in his life. But is that really true? Let's look at a few things in one day of Ovia's life. All of them have something to do with some type of government. Can you explain why?

6.00 am.

7.00 am.

4.30 pm.

5.00 pm.

6.00 am:	Ovia washes under the tap outside his house.
7.00 am:	He watches women share yams to sell some at the local market.
8.00 am:	Ovia listens to the headmaster speak to the school assembly.
8.30 am:	He receives a letter from his friend in Lae.
10.30 am:	Ovia and some friends are punished for not doing their homework.
2.00 pm:	Ovia is elected as the class captain for the year.
3.30 pm:	Ovia watches men fixing the road he uses every day.
4.30 pm:	Ovia's father tells him to chop firewood in preparation for dinner.
5.00 pm:	Ovia watches a village policeman break up a fight in the street.
8.00 pm:	Ovia listens to a meeting about bride price.

Government has a lot to do with your life too. You are sitting in class working because that is part of the way a school is governed. In fact, wherever people live together, there is some type of government.

Government is about the way people in groups organise themselves. It is about:

- choosing leaders to make decisions and organise activities,
- deciding how to use and share the group's resources,
- providing services to improve the lives of people,
- solving conflicts and punishing people who break rules.

Why Learn about Government?

Look at the envelope of the letter Ovia received from his friend. It shows you that Ovia is not just an individual person. He belongs to many groups and societies with different rules, different leaders, and different ways of doing things. He must learn how to live peacefully with other members of those groups. To do this, he needs to understand how they are governed. He needs to learn what he should do for his groups and what his groups should do for him.

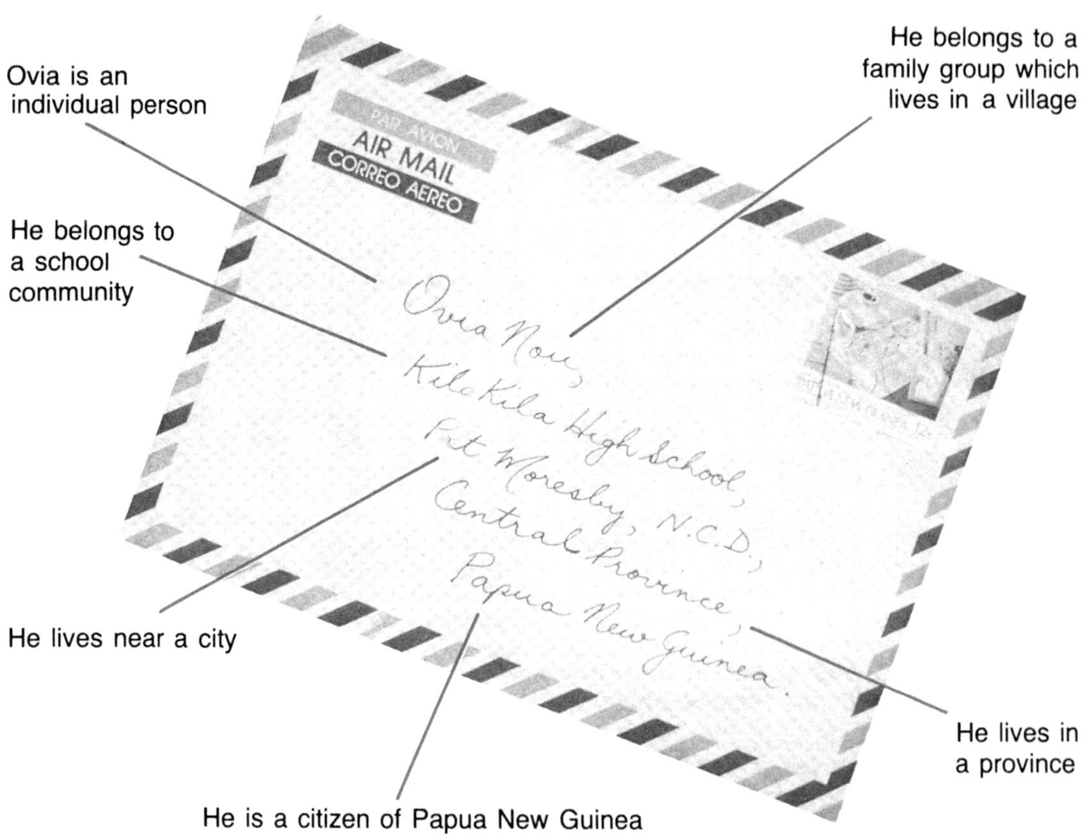

Ovia belongs to many groups.

Two Types of Government

Some of Ovia's groups are traditional ones. Others are new. These old and new groups have different types of government.

Traditional Government

Traditional governments have existed for thousands of years. In the past, groups such as tribes did not have much contact with each other and so different types of traditional government developed. Their rules and their ways of choosing leaders and organising activities were different. These governments worked well in their small societies. However there were no overall rules for contact between the different groups. Problems between groups were usually solved by tribal fighting and payback.

A Need for Change

During the late 1800s, contact with the outside world started to change things. You have learned how the island of New Guinea was divided into three parts by European countries. People began to mix with people from many different tribes and from other nations. A new type of government was needed to control contact between different groups and to introduce one set of rules for everybody in Papua New Guinea.

The New Type of Government

The foreign countries set up new governments which were very different from traditional governments. This new type of government was suited to large societies. In large societies, many people with different customs and ideas are joined together. A town and a nation are examples of large societies.

A Mixture of Both Types of Government

Most people today must know the ways of both types of government. In most villages, traditional government is still strong. In town areas, the new type of government is stronger and traditional ways are being forgotten.

A small society.

A large society.

The Work of Government

A main job of the government of any group is to try to satisfy the needs of its members. The job of satisfying the needs of all the individuals and groups in Papua New Guinea is too big a job for just one type of government. The diagram shows you that many groups satisfy Ovia's needs.

Needs satisfied by new government

Government:
- clean village
- sports field
- clean water
- roads
- school
- health clinic
- mail service
- protection by police etc.

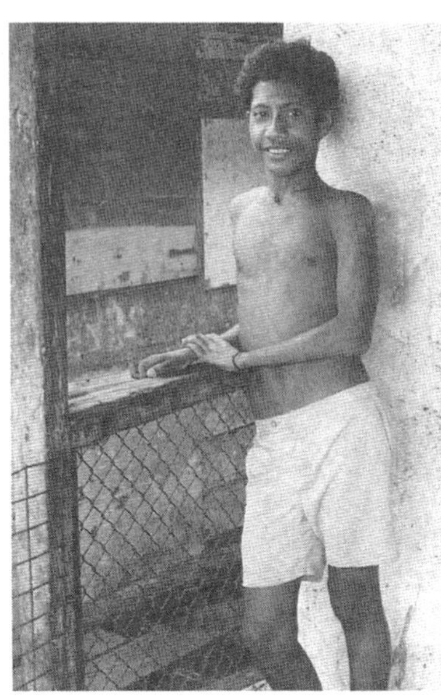

Needs satisfied by other groups

- food, clothing, house, love — Family
- land for gardens, help to pay bride price in the future — Clan
- traditional spiritual protection — Family and clan
- new spiritual needs — Church

Satisfying Ovia's needs.

Ovia's groups are like a series of circles around him protecting and helping him. The groups which usually have the strongest effect on Ovia's life are the ones which are closest to him—especially his family.

Family government is very important. When families are strong and work hard to satisfy their own needs, this helps the nation to be strong. You learned about family government earlier.

The next two layers of government are Ovia's clan and village. His village is in the Port Moresby city area of the Central Province of the nation of Papua New Guinea.

The outer layers of government around Ovia are the city, the province, and the nation.

Some groups in Ovia's life.

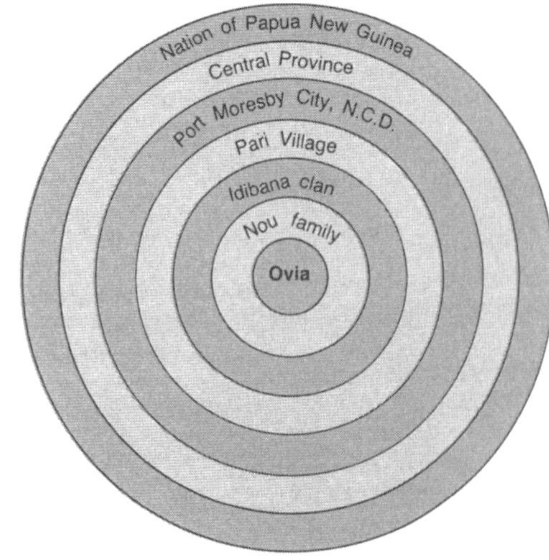

Ovia is like a dot at the centre of a set of circles. The bigger the circle, the bigger the group.

Levels of Government

The layers of government around Ovia are organised into **levels**. Different levels of government are needed to satisfy people's different needs. The next two chapters are about the **local** level of government.

Levels of government.

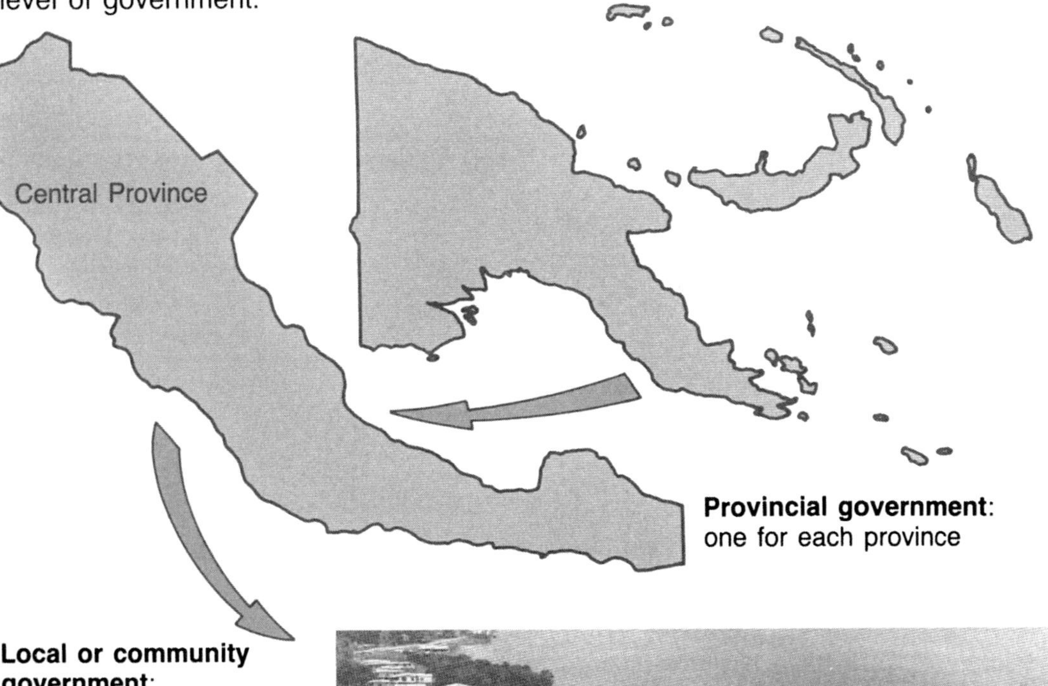

Ovia's village

Summary of Main Ideas

- All groups need some type of government.
- Government is about the way people in groups organise themselves.
- Governments must try to satisfy the needs of members of groups.
- Traditional governments suit small societies. The new government suits large societies.
- The new government has three levels to help satisfy people's needs.

Activities

Exercises

1. Write down five things that government is about.
2. What type of society does traditional government suit?
3. What type of society does the new type of government suit?
4. What is a main job of any type of government?
5. The new type of government is divided into three levels. What are they?

Things to Discuss

1. Look at the list on page 1. Explain how all these events in Ovia's life have something to do with some type of government.
2. Discuss the government of your school. Here are some things you could think about. Who are the leaders? How did they become leaders? Who makes the rules? Who punishes rule-breakers? Who controls the resources (such as money, food, books) of your school?

Things to Do

1. Write down a list of your main needs and how these needs are satisfied, e.g.

My Needs	How They Are Satisfied

2. Draw a diagram of yourself and your groups, like the one drawn for Ovia on page 4.

2. Traditional Government

We will learn about two types of government at the local level.

1. Traditional governments. These have existed for thousands of years.
2. Local Government Councils and community governments. These are a type of government introduced by foreigners.

Traditional Government

At school, Ovia has been learning about government. The students in his class come from different parts of Papua New Guinea. Ovia's teacher set them a homework assignment to find out about their own traditional governments.

Choosing Leaders

This is what Ovia's friend Kup from Western Highlands Province wrote about **choosing leaders:**

"This is about my uncle Kuma. He is a **bigman** in our village. He became a bigman by taking part in a **tei** or **moka**. This is a ceremony to exchange pigs and other gifts between bigmen of different clans. The bigmen do this to show their importance in public. Uncle Kuma is wealthy. He has three wives and many children. Being rich makes him respected. All the bigmen are recognised as leaders."

A moka or pig exchange in the Highlands.

Joseph from Central Province told the class about a different way of choosing leaders:

"I am from the Mekeo tribe. In our society, leadership is **hereditary**. This means the position of chief passes from father to son, usually to the eldest son. In the past we had two main types of chiefs. The civilian chief was a peace-maker and had to settle disputes. The military chief was the leader of war parties. Each chief had a sorcerer to help him do his work."

Civilian chief, war chief, and sorcerer.

Tomeda is from the Trobriand Islands. This is what he told the class about the **responsibilities of leaders:**

"My uncle Dogona is a hamlet leader and has many responsibilities. He must help organise dances and other activities for the whole village. He performs magic and organises the gardening. He is always ready to offer help and advice.

He also organises the ceremonies when someone dies. When my uncle is old he must choose someone from his own clan to take his place. Often nephews are a first choice. Uncle has already taught me some of the clan magic."

In the Trobriand Islands, a hamlet leader is responsible for gardening and many other aspects of daily life. (A hamlet is a small group of houses. Villages in the Trobriand Islands are made up of many hamlets spread over a wide area.)

This is what Ovia wrote:

"My village is very close to Port Moresby so our traditional ways have changed a lot. We still know who the village chief is but his position is not important now. The old people are sad when he is not invited as a guest to special events.

New types of leaders, such as the councillors, the pastor, and the village court officials are responsible for organising and controlling the village now.

One group of traditional laws we still keep are the laws about marriage and bride price payment. Family and clan leaders are still important in traditional activities like these.

The old people are sometimes sad to see the old ways changing. Nowadays young people sometimes argue with their elders. In the past, respect for elders was very important."

For the Motu people, bride price is an important part of traditional government.

Making Decisions

The class also discussed **how decisions were made**. They agreed that decisions were made in family, clan, or village meetings. Women were traditionally not allowed to join community meetings but they could influence family discussions.

Community meetings took a long time because everybody could give his opinion before the decision was made.

Sometimes decisions were made by **consensus**. Consensus is possible when people's opinions are similar and a general agreement is made.

Often people have different opinions and a true consensus cannot be reached. People argue with each other and try to persuade the meeting that they are right. When this happens the decision is made by **consultation** and **compromise**.

When a decision is made by **consultation**, the leader with most influence listens to all the other opinions and then makes the decision for the group.

In **compromise**, agreement is reached by each side giving up part of its claim.

Tribal co-operation depends on everyone being able to give his opinion. Here the men of Tambanum Village in East Sepik Province are holding a meeting. Women were traditionally banned from these meetings.

The discussion which the class enjoyed most was about **how conflicts were solved** and about **traditional methods of punishment**. The class agreed that the **payback system** should be stopped because often innocent people are killed or hurt. Some class members described how their people used **compensation payments** to settle conflicts. Ovia asked his grandfather about compensation payments in his village. The pictures show the examples his grandfather gave.

Two examples of compensation payments in Ovia's village.

Rules were usually obeyed because people believed that breaking the rules and customs would cause sickness, death, or bad luck. They also knew that they would be harshly punished and often shamed in public if they broke the rules.

These were just some of the interesting things that Ovia learned from his friends. The class agreed that traditional government works well for small communities where people grow up with the same beliefs, skills, rules and customs. They join together to make gardens, hunt, fish, build houses, trade with other groups, and protect each other. The government works well because it is based on strong feelings of kinship.

The class decided that some ways (aspects) of traditional government still work well today but that some aspects should be changed.

The villagers of Susuroka assembled for a marriage feast.

Sharing pork at a death payment in the Simbu province.

Kinship is a very important part of traditional government.

Summary of Main Ideas

- Traditional government still exists in Papua New Guinea.
- Different tribes had different types of traditional government.
- In traditional governments, decisions are made by reaching a consensus or settling for a compromise.
- Traditional government works well in small societies where people share the same culture and way of life.

Activities

Exercises

1. What were two ways that people became traditional leaders?
2. What are some responsibilities of a traditional leader?
3. How is a decision by consensus made?
4. What is compensation?

Things to Discuss

1. Discuss how Ovia could make a compromise in the following situation.

   Ovia's mother wants him to chop wood ready for the feast the next day. Ovia's friend wants him to play goalie in the youth club football match at the same time. How can a compromise be made?

   Discuss examples of decisions by compromise in your own lives or in the school.

2. Discuss the last sentence of this chapter. What are some ways of traditional government that still work well? What ways of traditional government do you think should be changed?

Things to Do

1. Write about traditional government in your own area. Use these headings:

   (a) How were leaders chosen?
   (b) What were some of the responsibilities of leaders?
   (c) How were decisions made?
   (d) How were conflicts solved?
   (e) What were some rules and punishments?
   (f) Is traditional government still strong in your area? How is it changing? Are traditional leaders still respected?

3. Local Government Councils and Community Government

History

Traditional governments satisfied the needs of the people for many thousands of years. Then in the 1880s foreigners introduced new ideas, new activities, and new types of government.

The top part of the time-line below shows that the time of colonial government was very short compared with the period of traditional government.

The bottom part of the time-line shows the types of local government there have been since the foreigners set up their type of government.

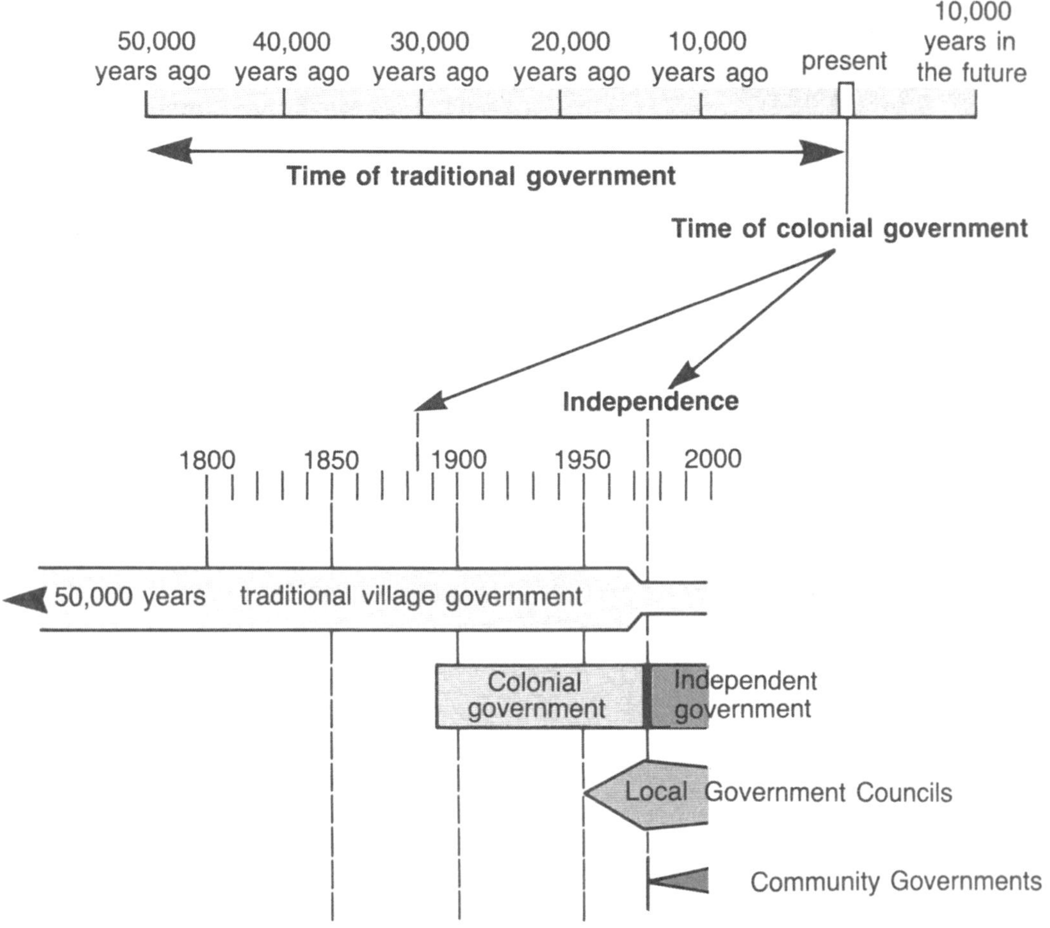

Local Government during Colonial Times

A main task of the early colonial governments was to try to keep peace between different local groups (such as clans and villages) and between the villagers and the foreigners. Both the British and the German governments did this by appointing government officers to teach village people about the new types of government in Port Moresby and Rabaul. These government officers were called **kiaps** in New Guinea and **patrol officers** in Papua. They appointed leaders in the villages to help them with their work. These new leaders were called **luluais** or **village constables**.

Many people helped the kiap do his work. However, the people had no direct influence over decisions being made by the new governments. Most of the time the new government did not affect the daily lives of the people. Matters to do with the new government became important only when the kiap made his visit. The rest of the time, life went on as usual.

A man wearing the uniform he used when he was a luluai.

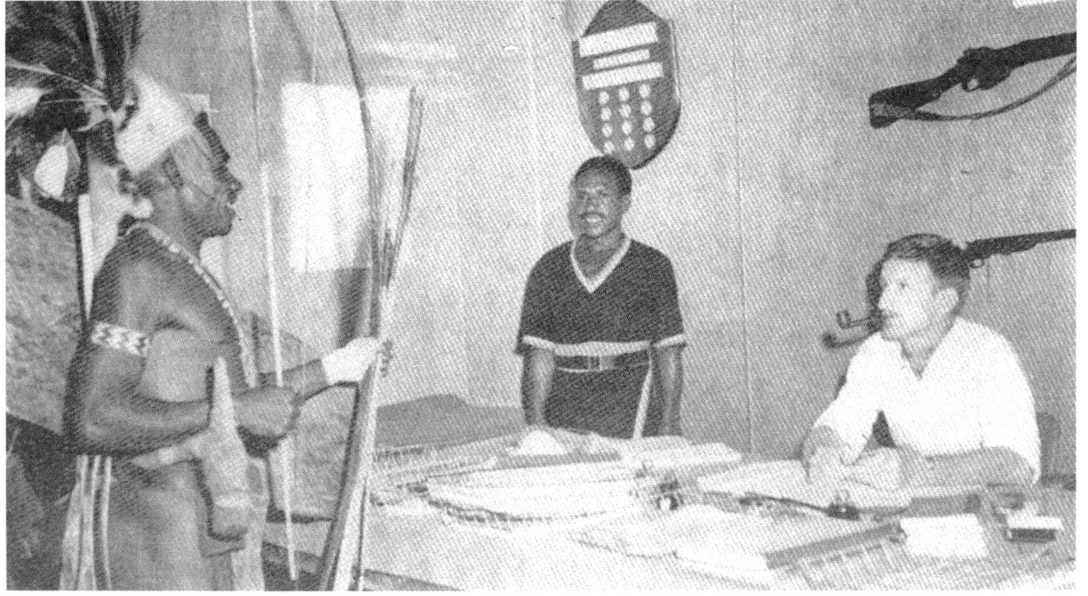

A patrol officer discussing the agricultural programme with a village luluai in traditional dress. The third man is an interpreter. (Lufa, Eastern Highlands)

Members of the Royal Papua New Guinea Constabulary.

"I think it was these senior members of the Royal Papua New Guinea Constabulary who more than any other group contributed to the pacification and extension of government control."

Fred Kaad, Government Officer.

Medical orderlies went with the kiaps on patrol.

Carriers on patrol.

During this time of kiap government the village people had their first contact with the new kind of government.

One problem with the colonial type of government was that it did not involve village people in making decisions. It was not until after the Second World War that the people became involved in the new government. In December 1949, a law called the Local Government Council Act was passed.

Special rules for organising meetings, parades, etc.

Most people do not know their leaders (impersonal government)

Saluting the flag, standing for the National Anthem etc. (paying loyalty to new symbols)

Many levels of leadership (hierarchy of control)

Special clothes for different jobs: uniforms etc.

Some features of the new government

Different people for different jobs: e.g. policeman, medical orderlies etc. (specialisation)

Filling in forms, reports etc. (written records)

The Growth and Work of Local Government Councils

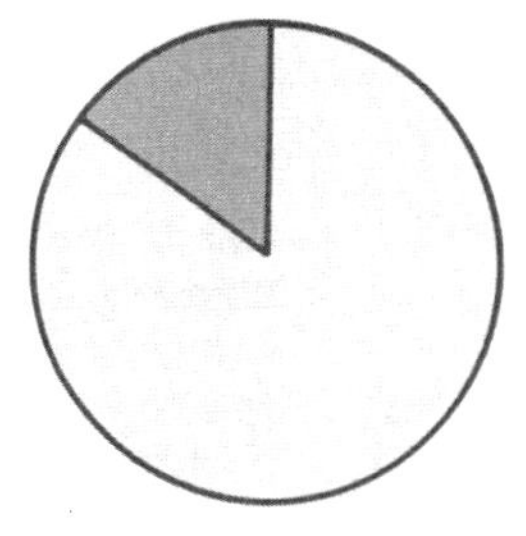

1952

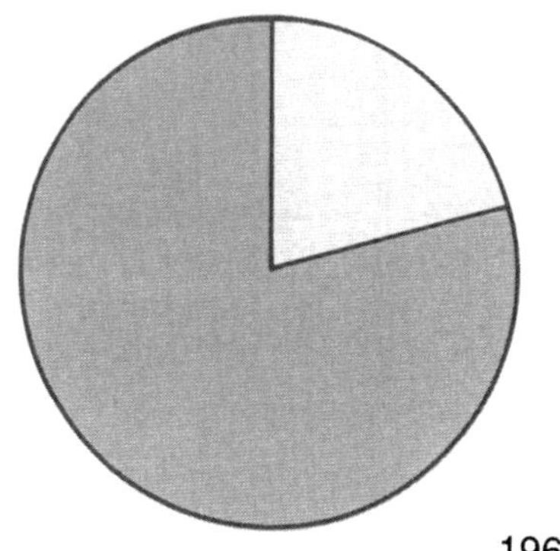

1968

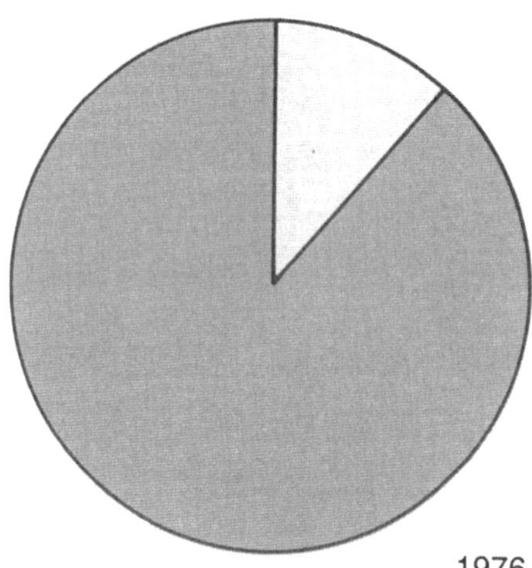

1976

The darker colour shows the proportion of the population under Local Government Councils. The size of the circles compares the total population for these three years.

Local Government Councils were important for election education campaigns.

People elected leaders to become councillors.

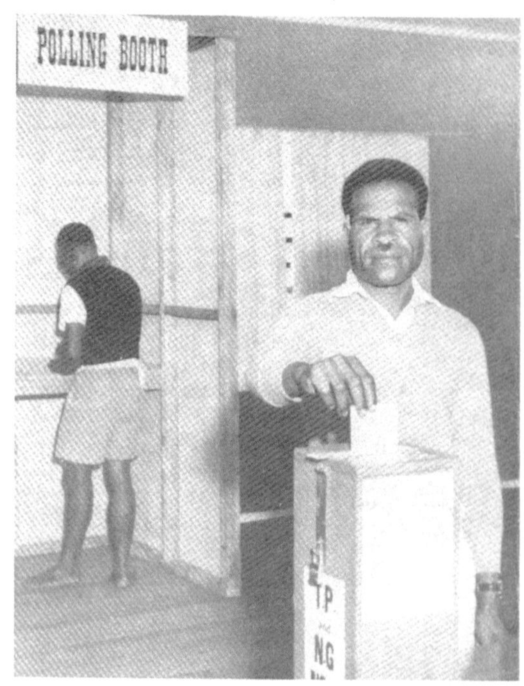

Voting at Goroka, 18 March 1961.

The Local Government Councils began to take the responsibility for some projects at the local level.

Building roads.

Providing water supply.

Agricultural development.

Some money for these projects was raised by collecting a Head Tax from each adult. The councils had to collect this tax. Each council paid a clerk to keep records of finance and projects.

Collecting head tax.

Counting head tax.

Council clerk keeping records of finance and projects.

Changes in Local Government since Independence

Before Independence, the national government controlled the local government council system. Since Independence this has been changing. The present situation is:

- Six provinces are still operating under the National Local Government Council Act (laws).
- Eleven provinces have set up their own Local Government Council Acts so they control their own local level of government. They use the National Government for advice or expert help if they need it.
- Four provinces have changed to community government. The idea of community government was started in the North Solomons Province. It breaks the local government councils into smaller groups. For example, in the past North Solomons had nine local government councils but it now has 37 community governments. An advantage of community governments is that more people can help make decisions at local level. A disadvantage is that it costs more to run because there are more governments. Each community government needs its own buildings and has its own staff.

How they get their money | **Work and how they spend their money**

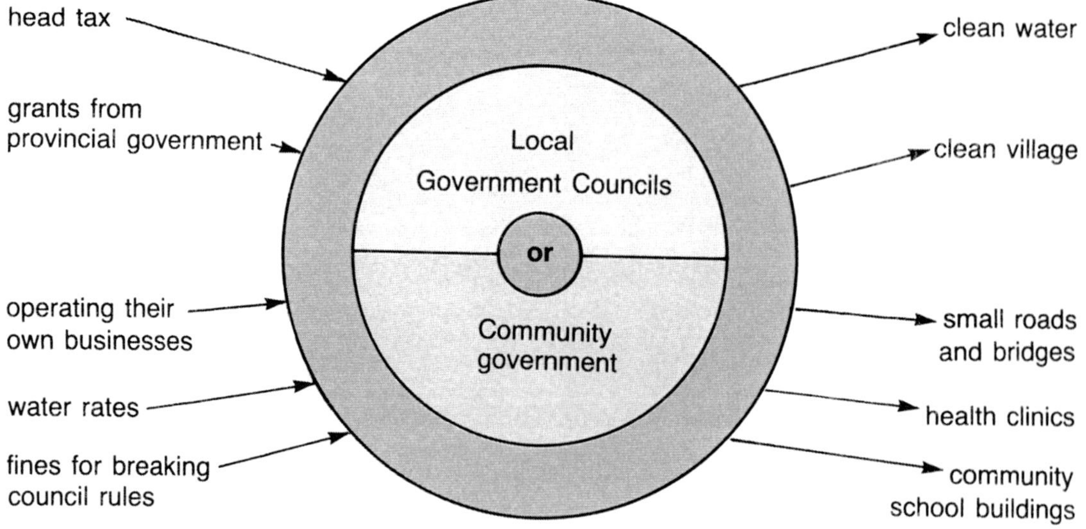

In the last two chapters you have learned about government of small groups at local level. The rest of the book is about government of large groups at provincial and national level.

Small groups and large groups have to be governed in different ways. The table shows why the government needs of small groups and large groups are different.

Organisation of Groups	
Small Groups	**Large Groups**
e.g. family clan village	e.g. town province nation
• few members	• many members
• fewer rules (usually unwritten)	• complicated rules (usually written)
• most people do the same type of work	• many different types of work
• most group members know one another	• most group members do not know one another

Summary of Main Ideas

- Small groups and large groups need different types of government.
- The colonial government introduced new types of local government.
- The kiap system took decision-making away from the people.
- In the local government council system people started making their own local decisions again.
- Since Independence, some local government councils have changed to community governments.

Activities

Exercises

1. What was a main task of the early colonial government?
2. What were the new village leaders in the colonial government called?
3. When was the first Local Government Council formed?
4. How were councillors chosen?
5. How is a Community Government different from a Local Government Council?

Things to Discuss

1. Discuss the ways that the new type of government was different from traditional government. (See page 17.)
2. Discuss reasons why small groups and large groups need different types of government. (See page 21.)

Things to Do

1. **(a)** Find out the names of the Local Government Councils or Community Governments in your province.

   (b) Choose **one** these and then find out:
   - how many councillors it has
   - how it raises its money
   - what projects it is doing
   - how often the members meet
   - how the members are chosen.

   (c) Invite a Councillor to talk to your class.

4. The Government of Large Groups

Government at provincial and national level is very complicated because provinces and nations are very large groups.

The diagram shows you some of the features of large groups.

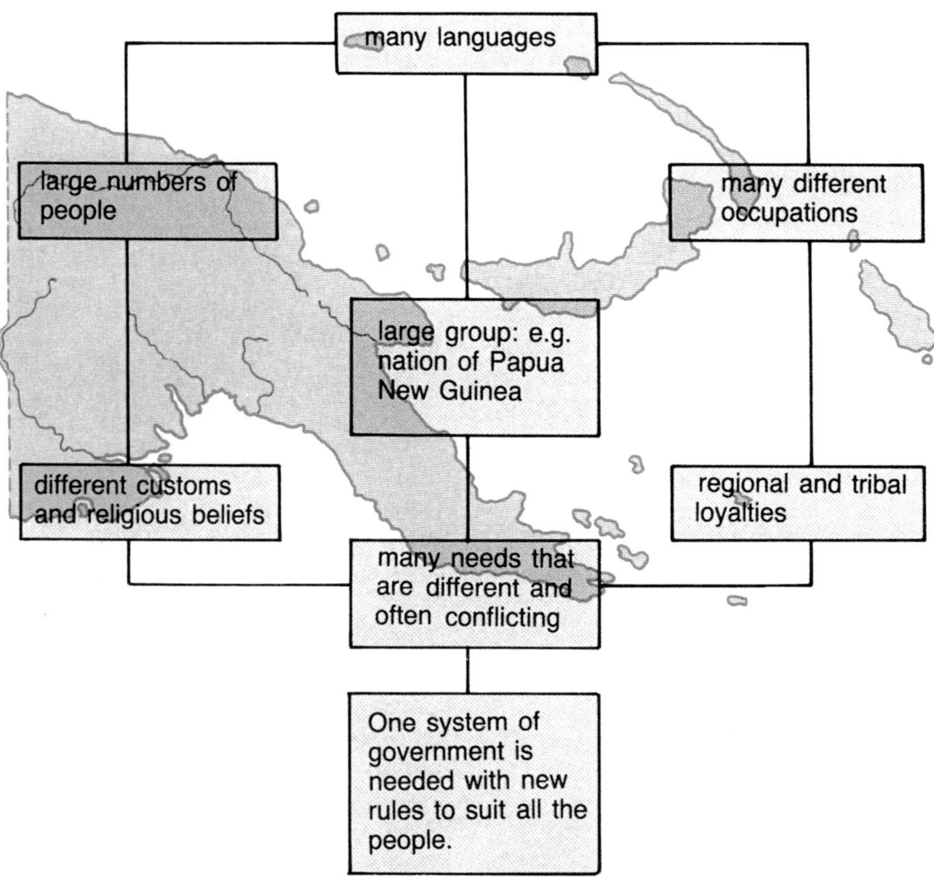

Some features of large groups.

Most traditional ways of government do not work well at provincial and national level. A new type of government is needed to join the many small groups together under one system. This helps to unite people as citizens of one nation. The new type of government is based on the Australian and British systems. Papua New Guinea's colonial government was also based on these systems.

Preparing for Independence

Before Independence, a group called the Constitutional Planning Committee had many meetings. Their job was to find out what type of government the people would want. From the ideas people gave them, this committee had to plan the best way to organise the government of the new nation. There were some disagreements, but, after all their research, they made many recommendations to the government at that time.

From these recommendations the Constitution was written. Soon after that, on 16 September 1975, Papua New Guinea became an independent nation.

The Papua New Guinea flag is raised on Independence Day, 16 September 1975.

During Independence celebrations, HRH Prince Charles unveiled a plaque marking the place where the new Parliament would be built.

The Constitution

The purpose of the Constitution is to give everyone in the country good government and also to protect them from bad government. It says how the government should be run. The Constitution also states what our leaders can and cannot do and it tells us about our rights and responsibilities as individuals. You will learn about these things later.

The Governor-General, Sir Kingsford Dibela. The Governor-General is the Queen's representative in Papua New Guinea.

The Head of State

There was some disagreement in the Constitutional Planning Committee about who should be the Head of State of the nation. The government decided that the Head of State of Britain should also be Papua New Guinea's Head of State. At present, Queen Elizabeth II is the Head of State of Britain. She lives in England. Someone must represent her here. This person is called the Governor-General. The Members of Parliament of Papua New Guinea recommend someone to the Queen for this position. The Governor-General is the ceremonial head of the nation.

The Work of Government

All types of government have three main things to do.

Make decisions, plans and rules. → Make sure these decisions and plans are carried out and rules are obeyed. → Solve any conflicts which occur and punish those who break the rules.

In small groups, these three things are often done by the same people (e.g. the parents in a family, or the elders in a village).

In large groups, however, if the same people did all three types of work they would have too much power. The Constitution says there should be three separate branches to do the work of government. This **separation of the powers of government** is one feature of the system of government called **democracy**.

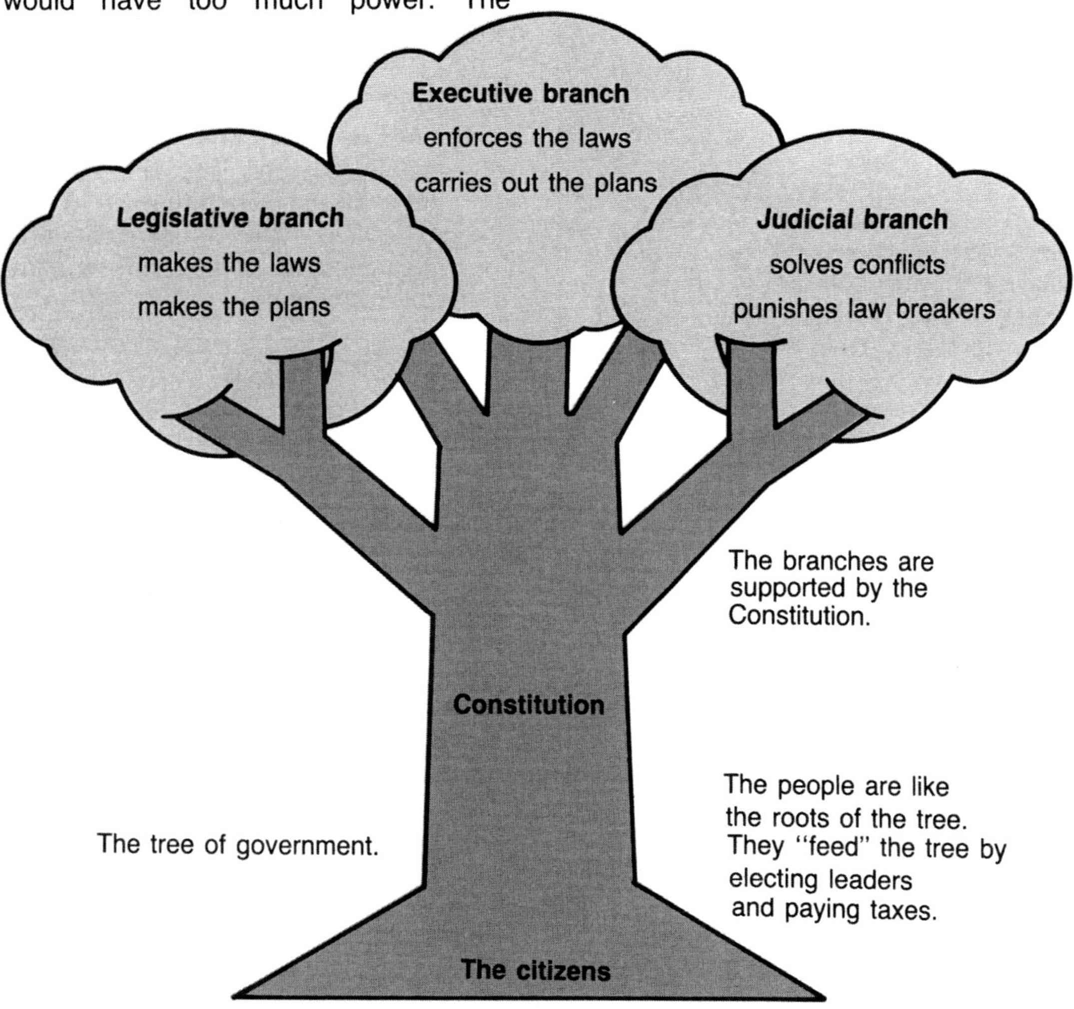

The tree of government.

Branches of Government

In general terms, these three branches of government are the **Parliament, Ministers and the Public Service**, and the **Courts**.

Parliament

This word comes from the French word "parler" which means "to speak". Parliament is the place where elected representatives speak for their people. They must tell Parliament about their people's problems and ideas.

Ministers and the Public Service

A Minister is a Member of Parliament with special powers. The Ministers are in charge of the Departments of the Public Service. They must make sure the Public Service carries out the plans made by Parliament.

The Courts

Judges and Magistrates work in the Courts. They must solve problems and punish people who break the laws made by Parliament.

This book is about the legislative branch of government. This is called Parliament. You will learn about the other branches of government later in the course.

The Legislative Branch of Government: Parliament

Members of Parliament are chosen by the citizens of the nation. They do this by **secret voting in an election**. This is another feature of **democracy**. At election time, politicians say many things and make promises which can be confusing. People must use their right to vote wisely.

Voting is an important democratic right.

Democracy

Voting is an important democratic right

Parliament

Representatives

ballot box

vote

People

People have the right to change leaders in elections

Democracy.

Dictatorship

In some countries people do not have this right

Dictator keeps power by force

armed men

people

People do not have the right to change government in elections

Dictatorship.

The election process.

The Political Party System

Most Members of Parliament belong to a **political party**. A political party is a group of people who have similar ideas about how a country should be run. Political parties are important at election time. Many candidates stand for elections with the support of a particular Party. The Party helps them in their political campaigning. The political parties which get many candidates elected become powerful in Parliament.

If there is more than one political party, people can choose. One party might win one election, govern for five years, and then lose the next election. This system of having **more than one political party** is another feature of **democracy**.

Politicians without parties might each pull in a different direction.

In a party they work together to reach a desired goal.

Political parties use special symbols, flags, posters, and badges to help persuade people to vote for them. Some people stand for elections without a party helping them. These people are called **Independents**.

Summary of Main Ideas

- Large groups need one system of government to suit all members of the society.
- The Constitution says how our country should be run.
- Papua New Guinea has a democratic government with:
  - the right to vote to choose leaders
  - the separation of the powers of government, and
  - the right to have a choice between different political parties.

What Do You Think?

One Party States: Some countries believe that having more than one political party divides the strength of a nation. In such countries, only one political party is allowed. One example is the Communist Party in the USSR; other examples are the Tanu Party in Tanzania and the UNIP Party in Zambia.

Activities

Exercises

1. Who is the Head of State of Papua New Guinea?
2. What are the three main things all types of government should do?
3. Name the three branches of government.
4. What is the work of each branch?
5. Write down three of the features of the system of government called **democracy**.

Things to Discuss

1. What is the Constitution? What is its purpose?
2. Why does traditional government not work well for large groups like provinces and nations? (Use the diagram on page 23 to help you.)
3. Discuss the advantages of the three features of democracy that you wrote down. Can you think of any disadvantages?

Things to Do

1. Organise your own elections for a class or school president. You will need to:

   (a) Form into Parties. Give your Party a name. Each Party chooses a candidate.
   (b) The candidate and his Party members plan their campaign policy and speech. Make posters etc. if you can.
   (c) Candidates make speeches at Assembly.
   (d) Voting is done by secret ballot. (Teachers will need to prepare the ballot papers.)
   (e) Counting the votes. You will need some students to act as Electoral Officers and some as Scrutineers for the candidates.

2. Look carefully at the drawings on page 28 and write down three facts about the **election process**.

5. National Parliament

The National Parliament is made up of 109 elected members. They are:

- 20 provincial members—one to represent each province. They are sometimes called Regional Members.
- 89 open members representing the smaller electorates within the provinces.

The table gives you some information about the electorates for National Parliament.

Areas, Population, and Electorates				
Province	**Approximate Area (sq. km)**	**Approximate Population**	**Open Electorates**	**Provincial Electorates**
Manus	1 940	26 000	1	1
Gulf	39 780	64 000	2	1
New Ireland	10 000	66 000	2	1
Northern (Oro)	22 200	77 000	2	1
Western (Fly)	97 600	79 000	3	1
West New Britain	20 500	89 000	2	1
West Sepik (Sandaun)	31 150	114 000	4	1
Central	32 120	117 000	4	1
Milne Bay	20 250	128 000	4	1
North Solomons	10 620	129 000	3	1
East New Britain	19 200	133 000	4	1
Enga	10 790	165 000	5	1
Simbu	5 880	178 000	6	1
Madang	29 150	211 000	6	1
East Sepik	44 000	222 000	6	1
Southern Highlands	12 000	236 000	8	1
Western Highlands	8 300	266 000	7	1
Eastern Highlands	14 200	277 000	8	1
Morobe	34 100	311 000	9	1
National Capital District	308	124 000	3	1
Total (19 provinces and NCD)			89	20

How is Parliament Organised?

After an election, the Members of Parliament form themselves into a Government and an Opposition. If more than half (**a majority**) of the members come from the same political party, then that party will form the **Government**. Its leader will usually become the **Prime Minister**. The rest of the members form the **Opposition**. One of them will be elected **Leader of the Opposition**.

Often one party on its own does not have a majority of members. When this happens, different parties join together to form a **coalition government**.

All of our national parliaments from Independence to 1986 have been coalition governments.

This pie graph shows the make-up of the first parliament after Independence.

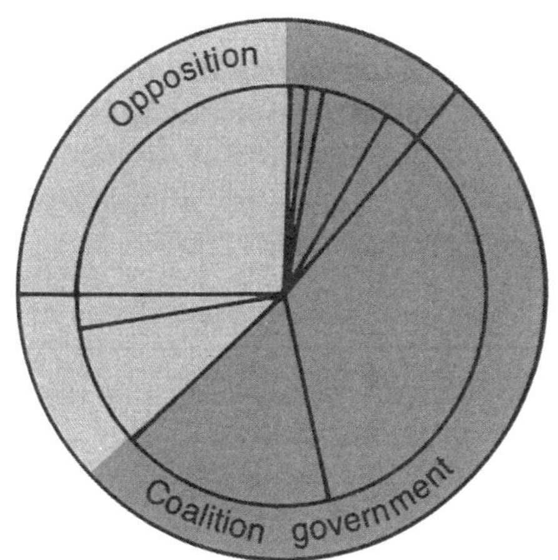

The chart below gives the changes in the Government and the Opposition between 1977 and 1986.

Paths to Power

Leader	Chan	Kwarara	Momis	Okuk	Somare	Torato	Wingti
Party	People's Progress Party	Papua Party	Melanesian Alliance	National Party	Pangu Pati	United Party	People's Democratic Movement

	Government	**Opposition**
Election 1977		
Vote of No-Confidence 1980		
Election 1982		
Vote of No-Confidence 1985		

Why is an Opposition Important?

The Opposition must make sure that the Government controls and develops the country fairly. The power that a Government has affects the people.

The Opposition has to try to make sure that the Government does things that are good for the people. The Opposition also provides a possible alternative government. A strong Opposition is an important part of democratic government.

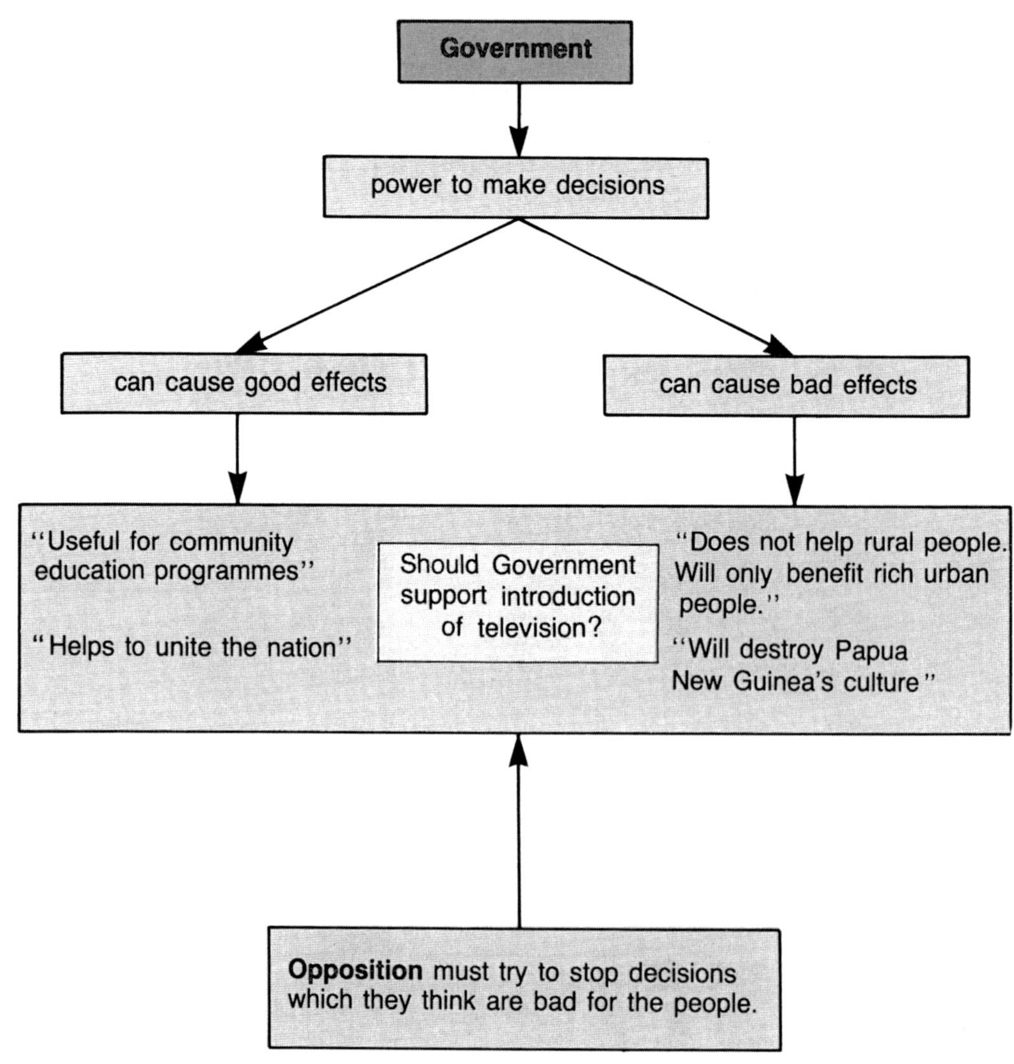

The National Executive Council

After the Government and Opposition have been formed, the Prime Minister chooses members from the Government to become his **Ministers**. This group of Ministers is called the **National Executive Council** (NEC). Each Minister is in charge of a government department such as Health, Education, Finance, and Primary Industry. The NEC is sometimes called Cabinet.

At the first meeting of Parliament after an election, all members vote to choose a **Speaker**. The Speaker acts as the chairman of the meetings of Parliament, and makes sure members follow the rules for discussion.

Sir John Guise was the first Papua New Guinean to become Speaker of Parliament. This was in 1968.

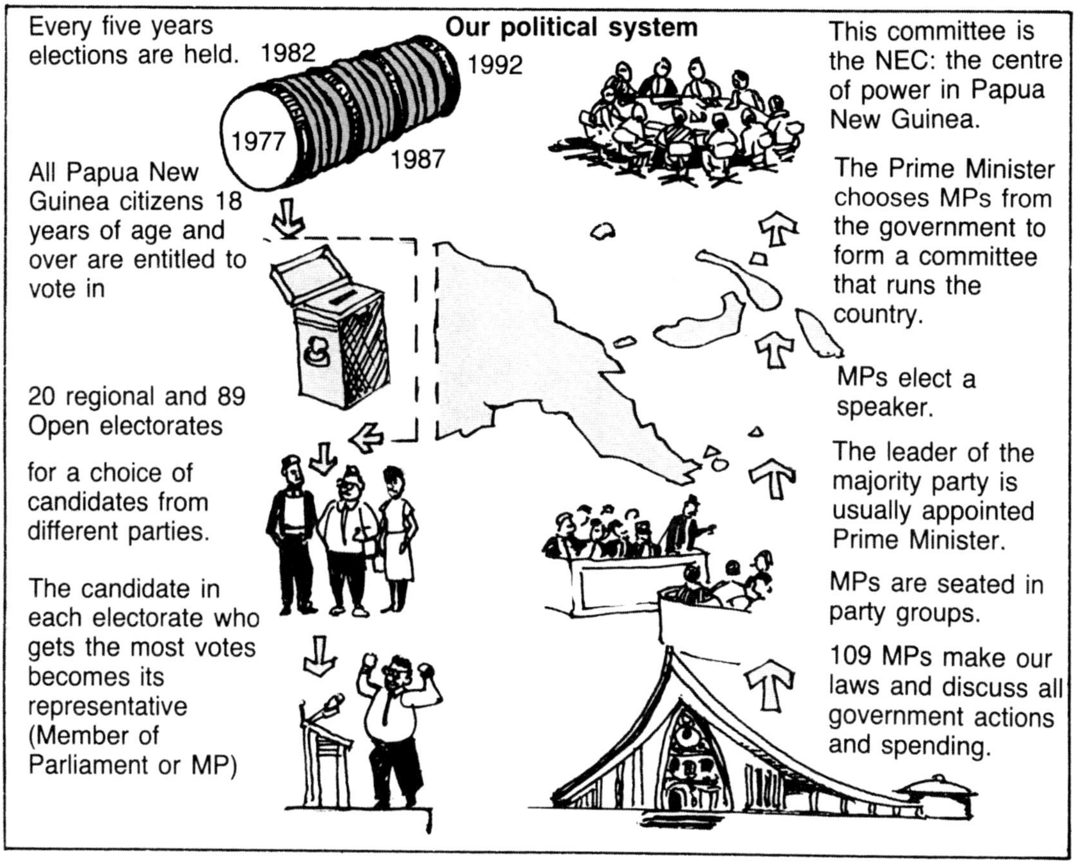

Our political system

Every five years elections are held. 1982 1992 1977 1987

All Papua New Guinea citizens 18 years of age and over are entitled to vote in

20 regional and 89 Open electorates

for a choice of candidates from different parties.

The candidate in each electorate who gets the most votes becomes its representative (Member of Parliament or MP)

109 MPs make our laws and discuss all government actions and spending.

MPs are seated in party groups.

The leader of the majority party is usually appointed Prime Minister.

MPs elect a speaker.

The Prime Minister chooses MPs from the government to form a committee that runs the country.

This committee is the NEC: the centre of power in Papua New Guinea.

The Work of National Parliament

The people of Papua New Guinea elect their members of National Parliament to do two main jobs.

1. They make decisions and plans about how the country should be run and developed, and about how resources should be shared.
2. They make and change the laws of the nation.

Parliament is the decision-making branch of government. Citizens give their representatives that power when they elect them. The work to carry out the decisions Parliament makes is done by the Public Service.

Road sealing soon

TWO main highways in East Sepik province will soon be considered for sealing.

WINGTI BLESSES OIL PALM PROJECT

A multi-million kina oil palm project in the Milne Bay Province was given the go-ahead yesterday by the Prime Minister Mr Paias Wingti.

WE ARE HERE TO SEE THAT EVERYBODY GETS A FAIR SHARE

Money for Oro

The Oro government has been reassured about K120,000 allocated by the National Planning Office to fund projects in the province.

PNG, INDONS TO CONSIDER TREATY

HOME SCHEME FLOATED WITH NEW DESIGN

THE government yesterday re-launched the National Home Ownership Scheme — a 1981 project which failed to get off the ground.

No timber royalties for the govt

THE Government yesterday rid itself from receiving timber royalties.

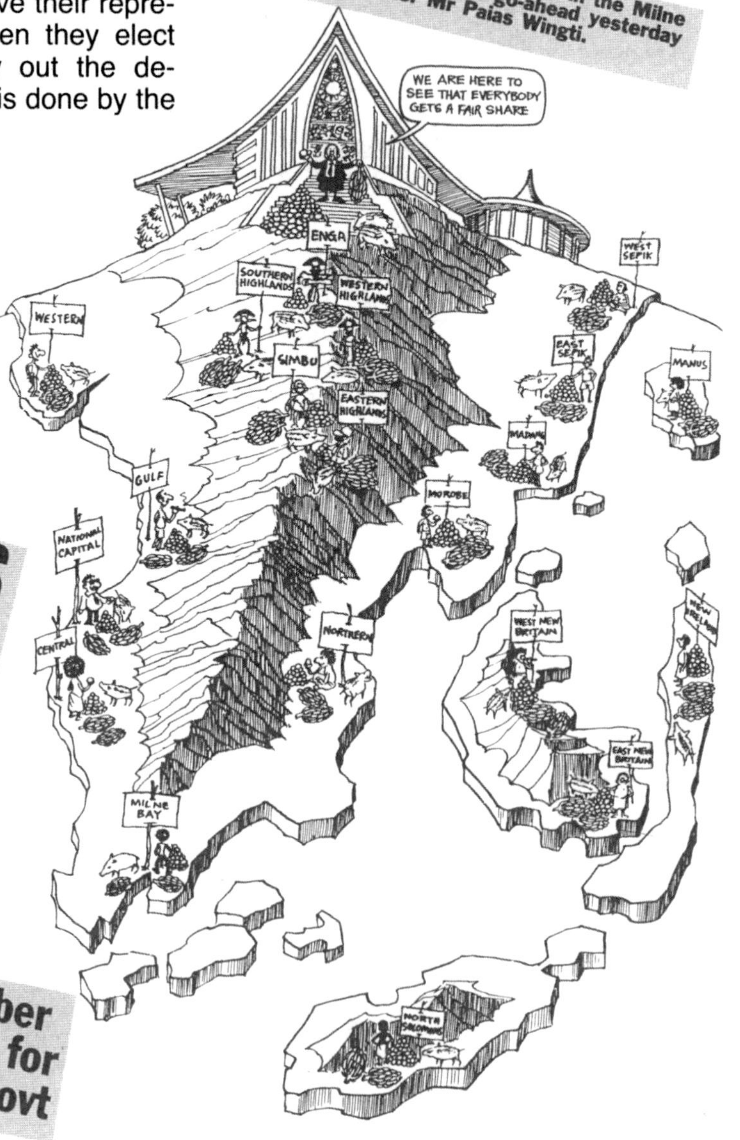

60 bills in the queue

The bills from last year that are are still before Parliament include the Correctional Service Bill 1984, the Industry Assistance Board 1984 and Village Courts (Amendment) 1983. Also before Parliament are the constitutional amendments on the Calling of Parliament Bill 1984 that were first debated on May 17 last year, Parliamentary Salaries ...nal Bill 1983 and Public Services Co... Bill 1984.

Budget will be passed: Wingti

PRIME Minister Mr Paias Wingti is optimistic that the 1986 revised Budget will be passed by Parliament next month.

Wingti acts as more coffee fungus found

Rush law to curb all travel

Legislation will be rushed through Parliament today to allow the Government to control the movement of Highlands people.

How parliament passes laws.

Stage 1. Complaints to Member of Parliament, or Ministers see need for a new law.

Stage 2. Lawyers research the Bill and prepare it for Parliament.

Stage 3. Parliament discusses the Bill (after 3 readings), then votes.

Stage 4. The Bill becomes law when the Speaker certifies (signs) it. Some laws cannot be used until they have been gazetted (published) by the Governor-General.

A Visit to National Parliament

Ovia and his friends chattered excitedly as they walked along the path towards the main block of Parliament. When they entered the door they became very quiet. The entrance room (foyer) is so big that they felt very small.

The Chamber and offices for the Speaker and Prime Minister are in this block.

They met the Sergeant-at-Arms, who is the Speaker's special helper. He told an attendant to show them the **Chambers** of Parliament. This is where the meetings (**Sessions**) of Parliament are held. The Members have special places to sit in the Chambers.

Opening of new Parliament House in August 1984.

The boys were shown the **Mace**. This is always put on the table when Parliament is in Session. This custom is from the British Parliament. A mace is a heavy stone fighting club. Long ago in Britain, the Sergeant-at-Arms always carried a mace to protect the King. Today the Mace is used as a symbol of the power and authority of Parliament.

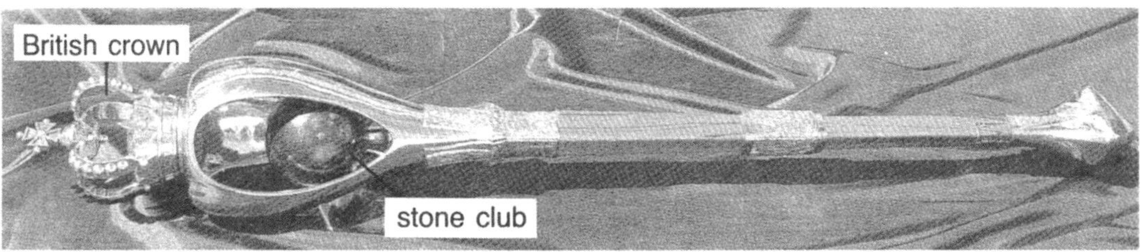

The Mace.

The boys then went to the other two blocks of the Parliament building. The second block has all the offices and working areas for the Members of Parliament. The third block has rooms for eating and relaxing after work.

The parliamentary library.

Members' diningroom.

Committee table where parliamentary committees meet to plan the work of parliament. Committee members can be from the Government or the Opposition. Ministers cannot be members of parliamentary committees.

A Minister's office.

As the boys walked to the PMV stop they looked up the hill and felt proud of their National Parliament. The style of buildings is like two types of traditional buildings. It is a new building for the new type of government but its design reminds us about the importance of our traditions.

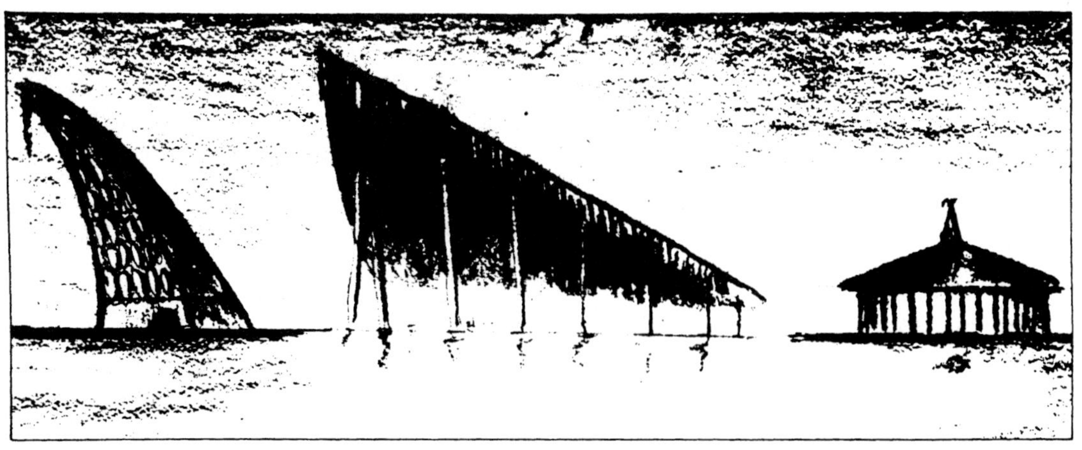

Summary of Main Ideas

- National Parliament has regional and open electorates. Provinces with more people have more Members of Parliament.
- Parliament has two major groups of Members—Government Members and Opposition Members.
- A strong Opposition is an important feature of democracy.
- Parliament decides how the country should be run and makes the laws of the nation.

Activities

Exercises

1. How many Members are there in National Parliament?
2. Members of Parliament are divided into two main groups. What are these groups?
3. What is a **coalition government**?
4. What do the letters **NEC** stand for? What is the NEC?

Things to Discuss

1. Why is an Opposition important? Collect newspaper articles about Government decisions. Discuss the good and bad effects of the decision. Do you think the Opposition should try to stop the decision?
2. Look at the chart called **Paths to Power** on page 33. Discuss the changes in the Government and Opposition since 1986. Is the present government a coalition government? What are the advantages and disadvantages of a coalition government?
3. Look at the **Work of Government** section.
   (a) Discuss what the cartoon about sharing wealth is trying to say.
   (b) Discuss whether the newspaper cuttings in this section are about planning or about law-making.

Things to Do

1. Answer these questions about the table on page 32.
   (a) Which province has the largest land area?
   (b) Which province has the smallest land area?
   (c) Which province has the highest population?
   (d) Which province has the lowest population?
   (e) Which province has the most open electorates?
2. Draw a map of Papua New Guinea showing the provinces and their main centres. In each province, write the total numbers of Members it has in National Parliament.
3. Write down the names of the Members of National Parliament from your province.
4. Write a heading **Who's Who in Parliament?** Under the heading prepare a list of names of Members of Parliament with special positions. Your list will look like this:

Position	**Name of Member of Parliament**
Speaker Prime Minister Leader of the Opposition Minister for Finance Minister for Education	

6. Provincial Government

History

Before Independence, in 1974 and early 1975, some leaders in Bougainville wanted to separate from the rest of the country and form an independent nation. Some leaders in other areas of the country were also asking for more control over the affairs of their own provinces.

The provincial government system was started to help solve these problems. Parliament changed the National Constitution to establish provincial government. In each province a special group of people called the Constituent Assembly prepared the Provincial Constitution. Over the next few years provincial governments were established in all provinces.

This change gave the provinces the power to organise and develop their own provinces. This is called **decentralisation of power**.

Dr Alexis Sarei speaking as Premier of the newly established Interim Provincial Assembly, North Solomons Province, 1976.

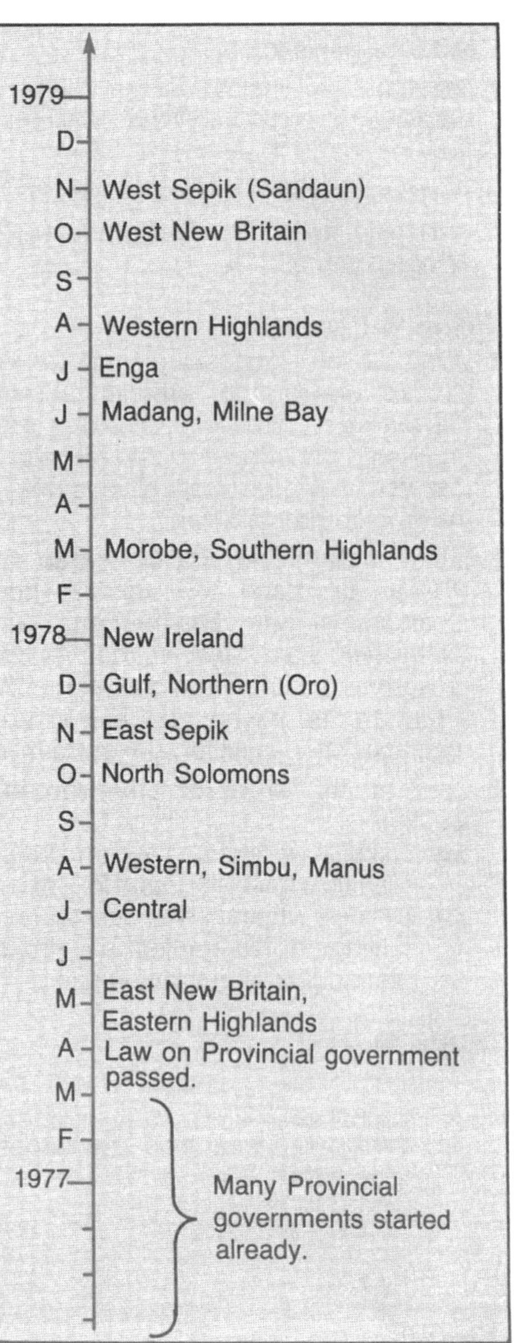

This time-line shows when the Constitutions of the provinces came into effect.

Opinions about Provincial Government

Ever since the start of the system of Provincial government, there have been many different opinions about it. Some of them are given below.

PREMIERS ALL WANT A SPLIT

Four Islands leaders back secession bid

The national government is too far from the village people. It does not know their needs.

Our country is very different in different places. Each area should have its own government.

Rubbish! There are too many governments in Papua New Guinea. Governments spend too much money on leaders!

United not divided!

Provinces should not have to share the income from their resources with the rest of the nation!

Yes! Provinces should make their own plans about how to develop their resources!

Papua New Guinea has too many politicians! Politicians do too much talking. We need workers.

National Parliament should suspend all provincial governments!

'NO BELIEF IN PROVINCIAL GOVT SYSTEM'

KOKODA people of Northern province believe the provincial government system is a waste of time and money.

A spokesman for the people told the Parliamentary Decentralisation committee in Popondetta yesterday that provincial governments should be abolished and replaced by local government councils.

The Structure of Provincial Government

Provincial government has the same structure as national government. There are three branches. They are shown in the table.

Structure of Provincial Government		
Legislative Branch	**Executive Branch**	**Judicial Branch**
Called the **Provincial Assembly**. Headed by the Speaker. The Assembly is divided into a Government and an Opposition. The leader of the government is the **Premier**.	Headed by the **Provincial Executive Council**, which consists of the Premier and his Ministers. Work done by the provincial public servants.	**Village Courts**. Provincial governments have the power to control the village court system. In fact, most provincial governments have not used this power. Most village courts are still controlled by the Village Courts Secretariat of the National Government.

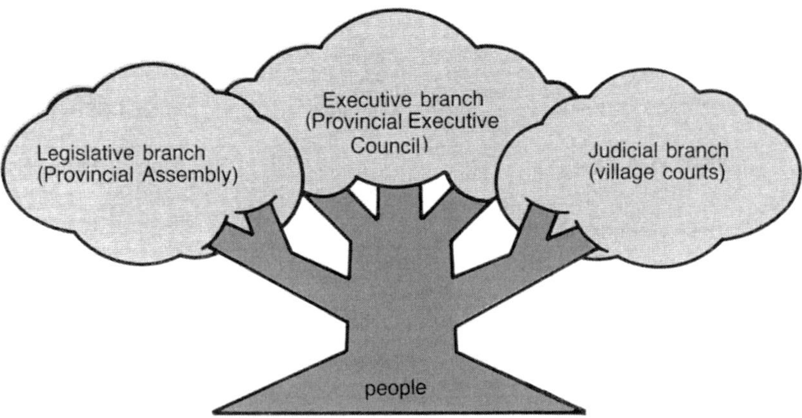

Like National Parliament, Provincial Assemblies have political groupings. This table shows the political parties of the Assemblies of the island provinces (1986).

Parties	Manus	NIP	WNBP	ENBP	NSP	Party Totals
Melanesian Alliance	3	2	3	8	19	35
PPP	2	10	2	5	4	19
Pangu	3	2	19	3		31
Others	4			2		6
Independent	2	6		4		12
Total	15	20	24	20	23	

Responsibilities of Provincial Government

Provincial governments have many responsibilities. The work for these is done by the **Divisions** (like Departments) of the provincial public service.

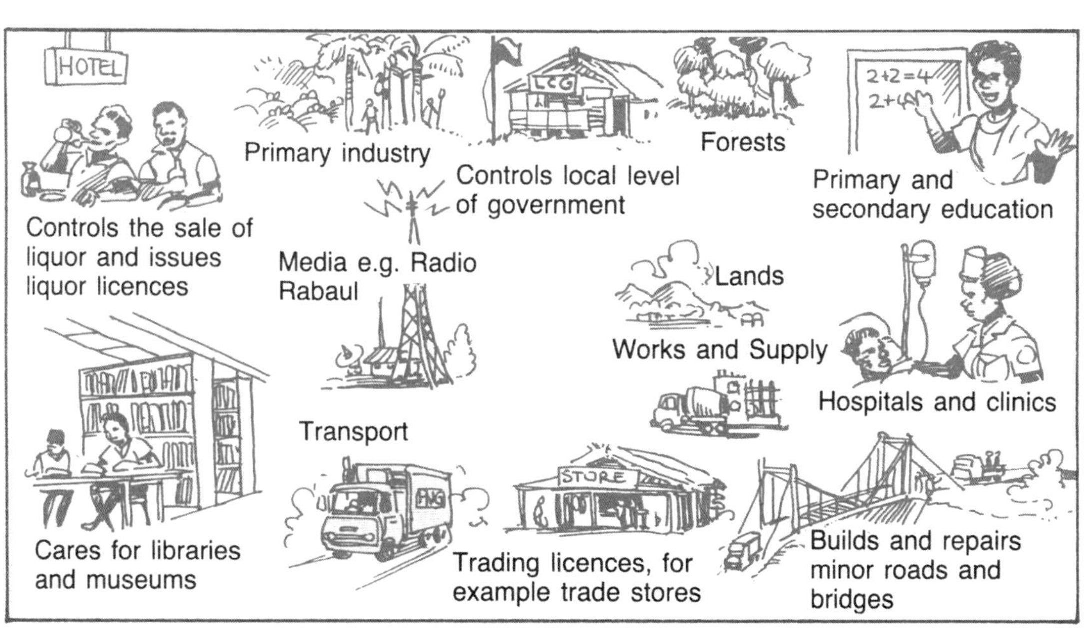

A lot of money is needed to do all this work. Provincial governments get their money in several ways.

Grant from National Government

Money from investments and businesses owned by the provincial government

Taxes (e.g. Sales, Entertainment, Hotels)

Money from court fees, and fines from village and local level courts

Licences (e.g. liquor, trading, hotels, guns, PMVs, dogs, etc.)

Provincial Government throughout the Nation

Each province has its own Constitution, flag, and crest or emblem.

Southern Highlands flag.

Emblem of Sandaun (West Sepik) Province.

Each province is divided into districts and smaller electorates to make it easier to serve the people.

Within the electorates there are also local government councils or community governments. The provincial government supervises the work of these governments too.

Each province is also important for different primary products and industries. The provincial governments and the national government work together to develop these resources. The map below shows some main centres, roads, and resources of Western Province.

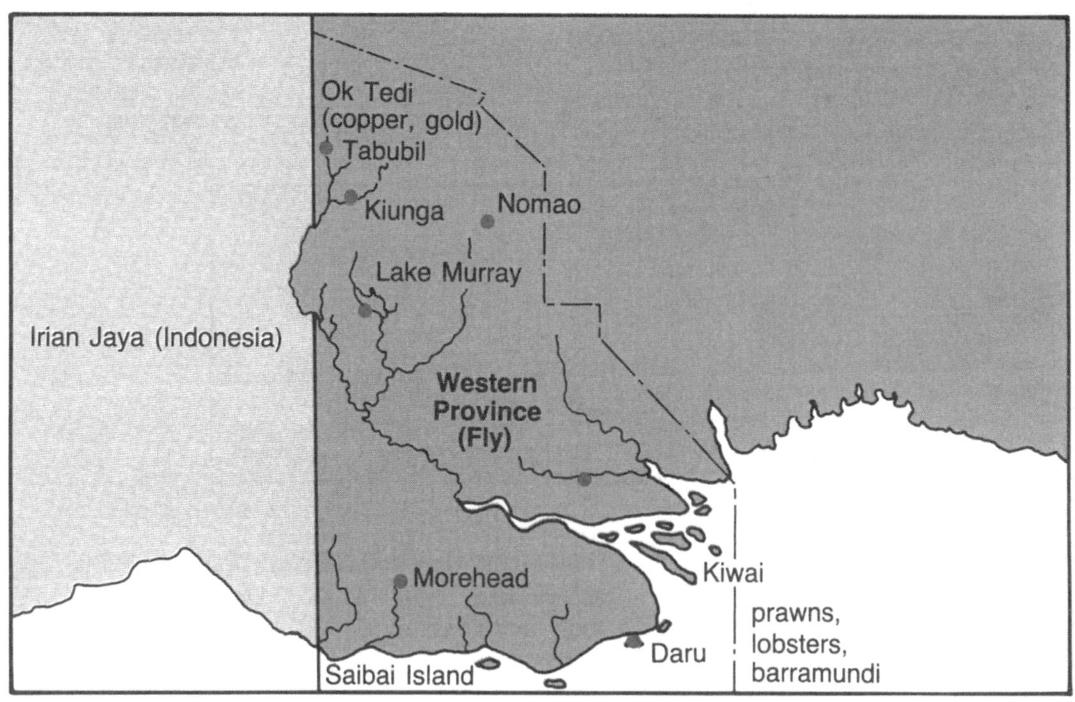

All provinces have the same structure of government with three branches. However, different provinces have different numbers of Members and Ministers in their Provincial Assemblies. Some provinces have also introduced new names. For example, the Morobe Provincial Assembly is called the Tutumang. The diagram below shows the structure of the East New Britain Provincial Government.

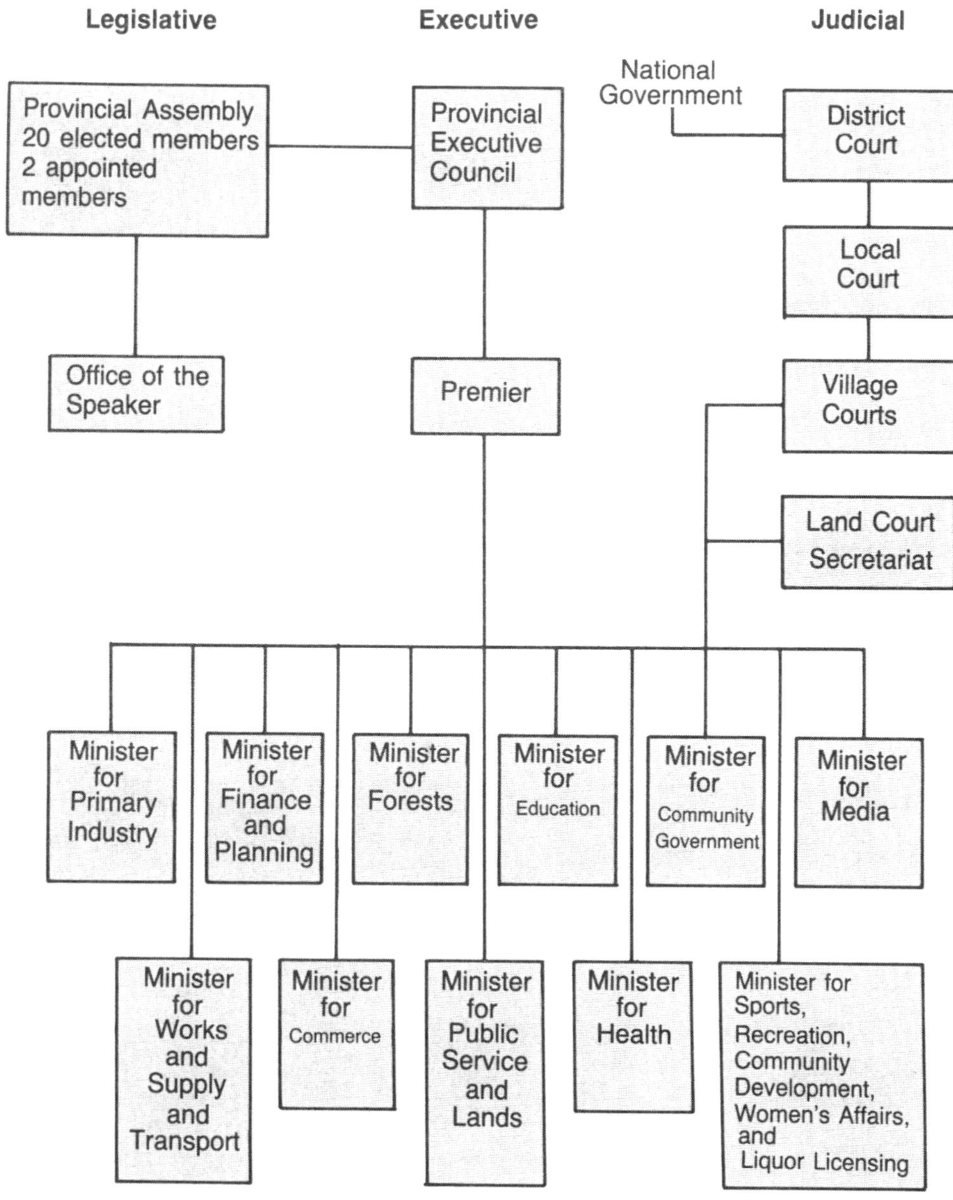

Provincial governments have the important job of looking after the special needs of their own provinces. Each province has its own projects and problems, as well as those which are common to the whole nation. Below are some examples of special projects or problems.

Joining forces

PEOPLE on Duke of York Island, East New Britain, have been told to help police fight crime.

The message was delivered by the provincial police chief, Superintendent John ToGuata, when he met with the island people at Molot government station.

His visit to Duke of York was prompted by an Easter fight between followers of the United Church and the Pentecostal Church.

The East Sepik Province has set up an elite team to scrutinise and negotiate all development projects in the province.

The premier, Mr Jonathan Sengi, said the 12-men team, appointed by the provincial executive council last month, would negotiate between the national and provincial governments, the resource owners, and developers.

Priority projects

THE New Guinea Islands Secretariat has promised to work bring all provinces to bring further together to bring further development to the region.

The provinces in past years have been used to actively sharing social, economic and agricultural developments.

These are some of the provincial projects additional to regular budgets, that have attracted national government funding for this year:

Manus

Projects:	1986 est. (cost in K thousands)
Health Boat	53.7
Rural Water Supply	25.0
Malaria Control	18.5
Rural Health	78.6
Total	172.8

New Ireland

Projects:	1986 est.
Rural Water Supplies	39.9
Malaria Control	44.9
Rural Health	54.9
Coastal Fisheries Development	20.8
Rubber Development	51.0
Community Education (for extra techers)	4.8
Sealing of Kavieng/Namatanai Road	60.0
Total:	276.6

East New Britain

Projects:	1986 est.
Rural Water Supplies	41.1
Malaria Control	99.3
Cocoa Rehabilitation	120.8
Extra teachers (Community Education)	12.1
Rural Health	100.00
Total:	373.3

West New Britain

Projects:	1986 est.
Rural Water Supplies	48.0
Malaria Control	131.8
Rural Health	97.3
Extra teachers	12.0
Rural Health	100.00
Total:	389.1

North Solomons

Projects:	1986 est.
Road upgrading programme	100.0
Rural Water Supply	50.0
Malaria Control	67.0
Extra school teachers	14.4
Total	375.6

Ne timbe deal

By LONELY FOMANI

LOGGING companies in Western Highlands must now provide essential services to landowners.

Lucas Roika, the Deputy Premier, announced the obligation at the official opening of an airstrip at Sipump.

Roads, schools and health services were to be included in future timber agreements.

"People who own timber would receive such services if a company began logging their timber," he said.

East Sepik to upgrade its schools

WEWAK: The provincial education board in East Sepik is re-advertising all the level 5 community school headmasters' positions in a bid to upgrade the standard of community school education in the province.

Urban Areas

Many provinces have towns large enough to have special groups to look after their needs. These groups are called councils, or commissions, or town community governments.

They have wider powers than local government councils. This is because urban areas have a larger and more varied population, need a lot of services, and there are a lot of complex jobs to be done.

Some of the responsibilities of town councils are shown in the diagram.

Town councillors make rules for their towns. If people break the rules they can be fined in court. The illustration shows you some rules made by the National Capital District Interim Commission.

Some of the responsibilities of town councils.

Town councils

Carries away rubbish and sewage

Water supply

Carries out health inspections

Cleans and tidies streets

Cares for cemeteries

Provides street lighting

Looks after sports grounds

Looks after public parks and gardens

look after our moresby

DON'T WASTE RUNNING WATER
DON'T DRINK IN PUBLIC PLACES
DON'T LIGHT FIRES CARELESSLY
DON'T CUT DOWN GOOD SHADY TREES
DON'T THROW LITTER ABOUT IN PUBLIC STREETS
DON'T SPIT OUT BETELNUT SPITTAL CARELESSLY
DON'T DUMP HOUSEHOLD REFUSE ALONG CITY ROADS

LOOK AFTER OUR MORESBY RULES
BY THE NATIONAL CAPITAL DISTRICT INTERIM COMMISSION

The Port Moresby Interim Committee pays these men to clean the streets.

Summary of Main Ideas

- Decentralisation has given some decision-making powers to provincial governments.
- The structure of provincial government is based on the national government system.
- Provincial governments also control the local level of government of both villages and towns.
- National government has the power to suspend provincial governments.

Activities

Exercises

1. Write down one reason why the system of provincial government was started.
2. What are the names of the three branches of provincial government?
3. Write down four responsibilities of provincial government.
4. Write down four ways that provincial governments raise their money.
5. Write down four responsibilities of town councils.
6. When did your Provincial Constitution come into effect? See if you can find out when your provincial government was actually started. It will be before your Provincial Constitution date.

Things to Discuss

1. Read the opinions about provincial government on page 43. Which ones are in favour of provincial government? Which ones are against provincial government? Do you agree with any of these opinions?

Things to Do

1. Prepare a class project about your own province. Your project should try to include:
   - **(a)** a map of your province,
   - **(b)** your provincial flag and emblem,
   - **(c)** the structure of your provincial government (see the diagram on page 47), with names of the Speaker, Premier, and Ministers,
   - **(d)** projects and developments in your province,
   - **(e)** newspaper cuttings about your province,
   - **(f)** problems in your province.
2. If possible arrange a visit to your provincial headquarters or invite one of your Provincial Members as a guest speaker about provincial government.

7. Conclusion

You have learned about government in Papua New Guinea—about the different levels of government and the structure and work of government.

Sometimes there are conflicts between different groups in government. Conflicts are a part of life and can even help development. The important thing is how conflicts are solved. Our Constitution says that "we reject violence and seek consensus as a means of solving our common problems".

The foundation of good government is **co-operation** and **compromise**. This is needed at all levels of society—from the individual person to the nation as a whole.

Each individual in a society must govern his or her own life wisely and show respect and concern for other people. The society will then be strong and peaceful.

In this book you have learned about government in Papua New Guinea. It is important to remember that government is about people. **The quality and strength of our nation depends on the people of Papua New Guinea.**

Co-operation: The school you are attending exists because of co-operation between the different levels of government.

Activities

Things to Do

1. Collect newspaper articles showing conflict and co-operation between levels of government. Make a class display and discuss the issues.

CONSTITUTION

of

THE INDEPENDENT STATE OF PAPUA NEW GUINEA.

PREAMBLE.

Adoption of Constitution.

WE, THE PEOPLE OF PAPUA NEW GUINEA—

- united in one nation
- pay homage to the memory of our ancestors—the source of our strength and origin of our combined heritage
- acknowledge the worthy customs and traditional wisdoms of our people—which have come down to us from generation to generation
- pledge ourselves to guard and pass on to those who come after us our noble traditions and the Christian principles that are ours now.

By authority of our inherent right as ancient, free and independent peoples

WE, THE PEOPLE, do now establish this sovereign nation and declare ourselves, under the guiding hand of God, to be the Independent State of Papua New Guinea.

AND WE ASSERT, by virtue of that authority

- that all power belongs to the people—acting through their duly elected representatives
- that respect for the dignity of the individual and community interdependence are basic principles of our society
- that we guard with our lives our national identity, integrity and self respect
- that we reject violence and seek consensus as a means of solving our common problems
- that our national wealth, won by honest, hard work be equitably shared by all

WE DO NOW THEREFORE DECLARE

that we, having resolved to enact a Constitution for the Independent State of Papua New Guinea

AND ACTING through our Constituent Assembly on 15 August 1975

HEREBY ESTABLISH, ADOPT and GIVE TO OURSELVES this Constitution to come into effect on Independence Day, that is 16 September 1975.

Glossary

Word	Page	Meaning
candidate	28	a person who is trying to win an election.
chamber	38	hall where Parliament meets.
citizens	2	members of a country.
clan	4	kinship groups.
coalition government	32	two or more political parties who form a government.
compensation payments	11	to give something in order to pay back.
compromise	10	agreement reached by each group giving up part of its claim.
conflicts	11	serious disagreements.
consensus	10	general agreement.
Constitution	24	the written rules which set out how a country should be governed.
consultation	10	talking together.
Court	26	the place where judges and magistrates decide if the rules made by the government have been broken.
culture	12	way of life.
customs	11	traditional ways of doing things.
decentralisation	42	giving some powers to lower levels of government.
democracy	25	a country governed by representatives elected by the people.
elect	26	to choose by voting.
Electoral roll	28	a list of all the people who are allowed to vote in an election.
electorate	32	an area represented by a Member of Parliament.
Government	1	the group of people who rule.
Head of State	24	ceremonial head of the country.
hereditary	8	passed on from parent to child.
Independents	30	politicians who don't belong to a political party.
judicial branch	25	the courts of law.
kiaps	15	patrol officers—government officers in colonial times.
kinship	11	blood relationship.
legislative branch	25	the law-making group.
levels	5	parts.
local level	5	village level.
luluais	15	village policemen.

Word	Page	Meaning
Mace	39	the heavy stone club which is the symbol of power and authority of Parliament.
majority	32	more than half of a group of people.
Minister	26	a Member of Parliament in charge of a government department.
National Executive Council	35	the Prime Minister and his Ministers.
opinions	10	points of view.
Opposition	32	the Members of Parliament who do not belong to the Government.
Parliament	26	law-making body in either a province or the nation.
political party	29	a group of people who have similar ideas about how a country should be run.
politicians	29	people involved in politics.
power	26	ability to control other people.
Provincial Assembly	44	the parliament of the provincial government.
Provincial Executive Council	44	The Premier of the province and his Ministers.
Public Service	26	all the departments which carry out the plans made by the government.
responsibilities	8	duties that someone is trusted to carry out.
rules	11	the way things must be done.
separation of powers	25	dividing the power between different groups.
session	38	full term of one elected Parliament.
Speaker	35	the Chairman of Parliament.
traditional government	3	government found in small societies.
village constables	15	village policemen.

Index

Central Province 1, 4, 5, 8
coalition government 32–3
colonial government 14–19
community government 14, 20–1
  money for 20
  work of 20
compensation payments 11
Constitution, the 24–5, 30, 42, 53

decision-making
  in National Parliament 36
  in provincial government 50
  in traditional government 10
  under colonial government 15, 17, 21
democracy 25, 27, 29–30, 34, 40
dictatorship 27

East New Britain Province 47
elections 18, 27–9, 35
  campaigns 28–9
  process 28, 35
electorates
  Open 32
  Provincial 32

Government, the 32–5, 40
government
  branches of 25–6, 44, 47
  clan 4
  colonial 14–19
  daily life and 1–2
  family 4
  function of 2, 4–5, 25
  in towns 3, 49–50
  in villages 3–4, 7
  levels of 5, 20–1, 46, 50, 52
  local 5, 14–22, 50
  new type of 3, 5, 7, 14–23
  of large groups 5, 21, 23, 25, 30
  of small groups 5, 12, 21, 25
  separation of powers of 25, 30, 44
  traditional 3, 5, 7–14, 23

Governor-General, the 24, 37

Head of State, the 24

Independence 24
  preparation for 18, 24
independents 30

law-making 35–7
leaders
  choosing 7–8, 27, 30
  responsibilities of 8
  under colonial government (luluais) 15
Local Government Councils 7, 14, 17–18
  increase in 18
  money for 19–20
  since Independence 20–1
  work of 19–20

ministers 26, 35, 44, 47
Morobe Province 47

National Executive Council (NEC) 35
national government 5, 23, 25–6, 46, 50
National Parliament 26
  building 38–40
  electorates 32, 40
  make-up of 32–3, 40
  work of 36–7, 40
North Solomons Province 20

Opposition, the 32–5, 40

political parties 29–30, 44
Prime Minister 32, 35
provinces
  area 32
  open electorates 32
  population 32
  Provincial electorates 32

Provincial government 5
  branches of 44
  ideas about 43
  history 42
  make-up of 45, 47
  money for 45
  work of 45–6, 48
public service 26, 36, 45
punishment
  traditional 1
  for breaking laws 25–6, 49

Sandaun Province 46
Southern Highlands Province 46
Speaker, the 35

traditional government 3, 5, 7–14
  change in 9, 11, 23
  decision-making in 10, 12
  kinship and 11, 12
  leaders in 7–8
  Mekeo 8
  Motu 9
  solving conflicts in 11
  Trobriand Islands 8
  Western Highlands Province 7

voting 18, 27, 30

Western Province 46